NORTH CAROLINA IS MY HOME

Charles Kuralt
and Loonis McGlohon

Edited by Patty Davis
The East Woods Press
Charlotte, North Carolina

Copyright 1986 by Fast & McMillan
Publishers, Inc.

Library of Congress Cataloging-in-
Publication Data

Kuralt, Charles, 1934-
   North Carolina is my home.

1. North Carolina—Social life and
customs.
2. North Carolina—Description
and travel—1981-
I. McGlohon, Loonis. II. Title.
F260.K87 1986   975.6   86-45579
ISBN 0-88742-107-5

To order your copy of the "North
Carolina Is My Home" recording,
please specify record or cassette,
mail $7.00 each (includes all taxes
and shipping costs) along with
shipping instructions to: Order
Department, EP700, P.O. Box 430,
Chapel Hill, NC 27514

Designed by Steve Galit Associates
            Charlotte, NC
Printed and bound in Hong Kong
by Everbest Printing Co. Ltd.

Published by The East Woods Press
            Fast & McMillan
            Publishers, Inc.
            429 East Boulevard
            Charlotte, NC 28203

2

Foster Scott

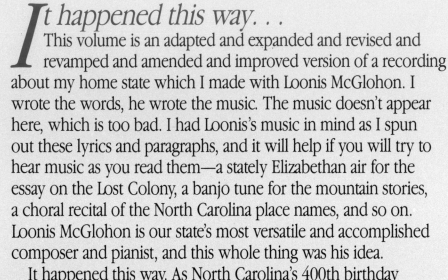

*I*t happened this way. . .

This volume is an adapted and expanded and revised and revamped and amended and improved version of a recording about my home state which I made with Loonis McGlohon. I wrote the words, he wrote the music. The music doesn't appear here, which is too bad. I had Loonis's music in mind as I spun out these lyrics and paragraphs, and it will help if you will try to hear music as you read them—a stately Elizabethan air for the essay on the Lost Colony, a banjo tune for the mountain stories, a choral recital of the North Carolina place names, and so on. Loonis McGlohon is our state's most versatile and accomplished composer and pianist, and this whole thing was his idea.

It happened this way. As North Carolina's 400th birthday approached, Gov. Jim Hunt got on the telephone and called everybody he could think of, urging some sort of contribution to the celebration. I was one of those he thought of. I called Loonis in Charlotte.

"I just got a phone call from Gov. Hunt," I said.

"I know. So did I," Loonis said.

"You got any ideas?" I asked.

"Sure," Loonis said, "we'll make a record. We'll give it to all the schools and libraries."

"I can't sing," I said.

"Right," said Loonis (who had heard me sing), "but you can type. Start typing."

"What'll I type about?" I asked him.

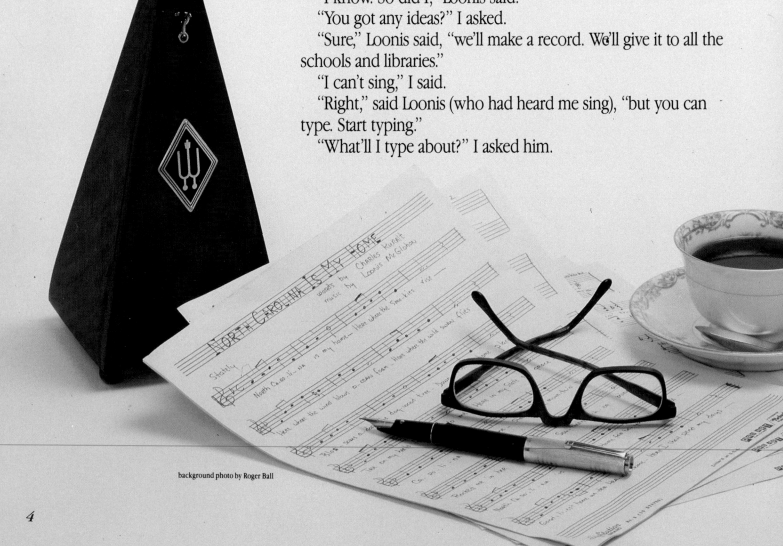

background photo by Roger Ball

4

"The mountains," Loonis said, "the shore. Barbecue, moonshine, pine trees, Thomas Wolfe, wild swans, tobacco barns, textile mills, all that stuff. You know."

I sat down at my typewriter and did as I was told. Loonis sat down at his piano and started writing music. We put the words and music together by letter and by telephone.

"North Carolina needs a new state song," Loonis said on the telephone one day. "Nobody can sing the old one. So I've written a new one. Listen." He put the phone down on the piano and played me a beautiful anthem. "I've got the title," he said when he had finished playing, "'North Carolina Is My Home.' You write the rest of the words." So I did. Somebody has actually introduced a bill in the Legislature to make it the new state song. I will always be amazed by Loonis McGlohon.

Hugh Morton

Loonis rounded up a few dozen of his friends—conductor and arranger Billy VerPlanck; the great banjo and guitar player Eric Weissberg; three of the most sought-after singers on earth, Marlene VerPlanck, Mary Mayo and Jim Campbell; and about half the New York Philharmonic's strings and horns and woodwinds; and we made the recording in four days in July, 1985. Charles Heatherly of the North Carolina Department of Travel and Tourism persuaded Piedmont Airlines to pick up the bill for the recording and distribution of the album, and it was sent to all the schools and libraries of the state, just as Loonis had suggested in our first conversation.

Here are the words. Please let your imagination supply the music.

Charles Kuralt

*T*here ought to be a book . . .

The passing of more than three or four weeks' time always produces lapses in my film of memory, but it was over lunch one day back in 1983, I think, when Charles Kuralt and I began to discuss a project called NORTH CAROLINA IS MY HOME.

Governor Jim Hunt had asked Charles and me to contribute something to the 400th birthday of our home state, an anniversary celebrating the 1584 settling of the colony on Roanoke Island.

The prospect of collaborating with Charles Kuralt was very exciting for me. I have been a fan of Charles ever since he wrote for The Charlotte News and read news on WBT radio back in high school. The fact that he was, and is, many years younger than I am dispels any notion that a hero has to be older. We knew he was talented back in those days, and he just keeps getting better. There are many good writers, and many men are blessed with wonderfully resonant voices. But none has the Kuralt combination—putting just the right words together and then having a great voice with which to say them.

Excited as I was about the possibility of working on a project with him, catching Charles Kuralt in between "On The Road" travels is like trying to trap a firefly while the sun is in your eyes. You can't find him! Somehow, in between Apalachicola, Florida, and Conshohocken, Pennsylvania, when he stopped at a pay phone to check in with his secretary, Karen Beckers, she added my name to the list of people trying to reach him. We set up a date for lunch.

Governor Hunt had not mentioned a specific idea for us. Certainly Charles Kuralt would need no help from me in writing a book. He doesn't sing, so accompanying him in "An Evening of Songs with Charles Kuralt and Friend" at the Governor's Mansion would not be practical. Charles is a great lyricist, as I learned back when we wrote his "On The Road" television theme, but even if I were to write a tune for the 400th birthday, who would perform it? And where?

I don't remember which of us came up with the idea of making a record. But we did decide that Charles would write some pieces about North Carolina and that I would put some music to them. If the project turned out pretty well, we would record it. Then we would request that the resulting album be given to every school in the state.

NORTH CAROLINA IS MY HOME
words by Charles Kuralt
music by Loonis McGlohon

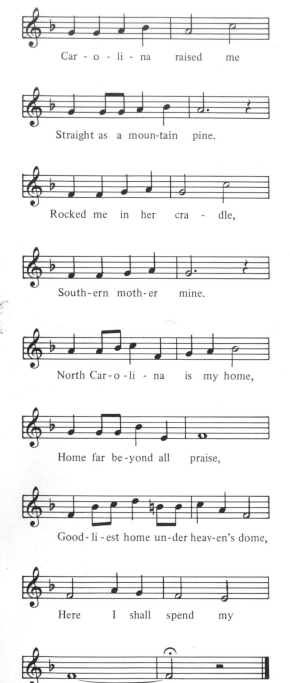

Car - o - li - na raised me

Straight as a moun-tain pine.

Rocked me in her cra - dle,

South-ern moth-er mine.

North Car-o -li - na is my home,

Home far be -yond all praise,

Good - li -est home un-der heav-en's dome,

Here I shall spend my

days. _____

The first piece Charles completed and sent to me was "Roanoke." As soon as I read the first page, I grabbed a sheet of manuscript paper and headed for the piano to start writing.

The second piece, "Backroads & Byways," was a bigger challenge. When you examine Charles' text on this piece it becomes apparent how much homework and research he did—matching rhymes and turning up little-known anecdotes about the towns and crossroads which North Carolinians call home.

Charles, for whatever reason, overlooked my home town, Ayden, when he was writing those rhymes. Now how could he leave out Ayden, the Collard Capital of the World? When I wrote him, scolding him for the omission, I included my own bit of homework, rhyming Ayden with Baden and Maiden. I will take credit for that one line.

Other than that, Charles did not leave out much of anything we love about North Carolina. Of course, he is too young to have gone to one of the first "air cooled" theatres where you watched a movie like "Frankenstein" and couldn't decide whether it was Karloff or the damp cold air blown around in the theatre which chilled a body to the bone. Nor would Charles remember the excitement we had watching a ten-story skyscraper climb above Kinston's main street. Charles doesn't mention having tasted shad stew on the banks of Contentnea Creek, but he does pay homage to country ham, barbecue and collard greens. And that makes things right.

"The Farmer" is my favorite piece in the collection. When this was recorded in New York in July, 1985, there were no dry eyes around the studio and control room. By the time Charles read the second paragraph, everyone within the sound of his voice was reaching for a handkerchief. The memories he recalls live in each of us, but few of us can describe them with such clarity and affection.

Someone, listening to the album for the first time, said, "These words from Charles Kuralt should be in a book to be read and enjoyed over and over." I think that was a fine suggestion. We hope you'll agree.

Carolina Memories

From where I sit, on the broad porch of the home of my mother and father, I can see down Jean Guite Creek to to Currituck Sound. The sun warms my shoulders, a breeze whispers through the pines, a great blue heron flaps across the water toward the marsh.

I have been gone a long time, but now I am home.

I have seen much of every state, and lingered on every continent, and always, always, I have been aware that I am merely a North Carolinian traveling outside my native borders. To come back to Dare County (300 square miles of land, 1200 square miles of water), and to take off my tie (for a tie is necessary in tidewater North Carolina only for going to church), and to relax into the ministrations of my parents ("Better have another one of those biscuits, Charles—they'll go to waste.") is to return to innocence, to ease, to Eden.

From my earliest childhood, the names of Dare County places, those strange and evocative names—Kitty Hawk, Nag's Head, Kill Devil Hills, Whalebone Junction, Jockey's Ridge and Seven Sisters—have thrilled me and filled me with wonder.

Foster Scott

Not far from my parents' porch, a highway brings tourists from faraway places here to the beach. Their cars come loaded with ice chests and fishing poles, surfboards and children itching to build sand castles. They will bask in today's sun. But they have no memories of all the yesterdays that make North Carolina so precious to me, and to other North Carolinians like me. The reality of any place is what its people remember of it. . . .

I'll always be glad I have seen the shrimp boats leaving Beaufort with the sun coming up. And I'll always remember the sudden chill of night coming early to the coves in the mountains, while the ridges above were still bright with day.

I remember the red gullies, the broomstraw, the fields of cornstubble in the Mecklenburg November, and in spring, the daffodils that still bloom by the hundreds under a certain Orange County oak. I remember mills with blue windows, and monuments to Confederate soldiers in sleepy courthouse squares.

North Carolina Division of Travel & Tourism

I remember bobolinks and buntings, and mockingbirds mocking, loblolly pines and live oaks hung with moss, the taste of scuppernongs from vines my father planted.

I remember making a slingshot from the fork of a persimmon tree and hunting rabbits with it along the creek bed. Those rabbits were as safe as if they'd been in their mothers' arms. I never hit a one.

Hugh Morton

Of course, it is all changed, or changing. I lived in the country outside Charlotte for many years. The deep woods my brother and I explored, certain that we were the first human beings to know these rabbit paths and clear streams—except, perhaps, for the Indians long ago—those woods are gone, the rabbit paths are residential streets with sidewalks and fire hydrants, and the streams have vanished into culverts underground.

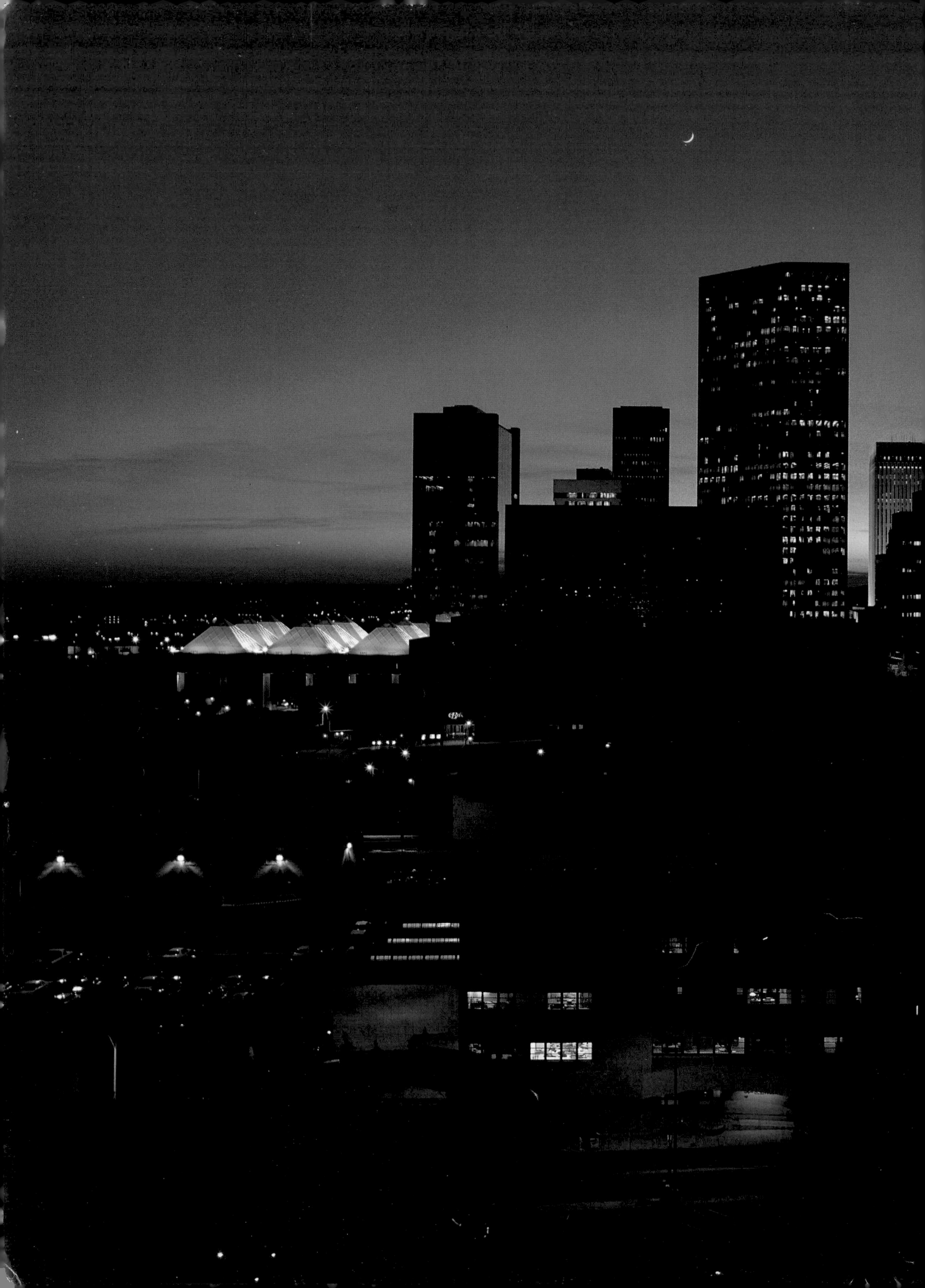

The cranes and the bulldozers do their work. Those who look back on our state as it is becoming will have great cities to talk about and sing about—skyscrapers, six-lane highways, microchips and megagrowth and jet planes leaving contrails on a sky of Carolina blue.

North Carolina is 503 miles from east to west, and 187 miles from north to south, so that leaves plenty of room for growth and change. Still, I am glad I know it as it is, and remember it as it was.

Have you ever stepped on a sandspur, barefooted? Then you must be from down home, too!

Carolista Golden

New moon over Charlotte.

Roger Ball

19

Roanoke

On a morning in July of the year 1584, two English gentlemen in armor, accompanied by soldiers, well armed, stepped into a small boat from the great ship in which they had crossed the Atlantic. They had come from England, the noble England of Elizabeth and Shakespeare and Sir Francis Drake, sent hither by Sir Walter Raleigh, favorite of the Queen. Sunlight flashed from their helmets as their boat was rowed toward shore.

The Elizabeth II, built for North Carolina's 400th birthday celebration.

Clay Nolen, North Carolina Division of Travel & Tourism

A single Indian stood on the sandy beach awaiting the men from the ship. He was silent, unarmed and alone, ". . .never making," one of the Englishmen said, "any show of fear or doubt." After they had stepped ashore, this lone man spoke to them gravely for several minutes. They knew it was a speech of welcome. At length, the Indian went to his own canoe, paddled out into the water and began fishing. When he had filled his boat with fish, he returned to the shore, piled his catch on the beach and indicated by gestures that the fish were for the Englishmen. Then he vanished.

The manner of their fishing.

22

SECOTAN
Dasamonquepeuc
Roanoac
Hatorasck
Pasquenoke
WEAPEMEQC
Trinety Harbor

"The natives are very handsome and goodly people," one of the Englishmen wrote in his notes, "and in their behaviour as mannerly and civil as any of Europe."

The Englishmen took his fish, and claimed his continent.

English America began there, on a North Carolina beach. The next summer, and the next, English ships returned, bringing soldiers and scientists and surveyors...and finally..settlers.

We know their names:
Christopher Cooper,
John Bright,
William Waters.
They are names like our names:
Margaret Lawrence,
Rose Payne,
Jane Jones.

William A. Bake

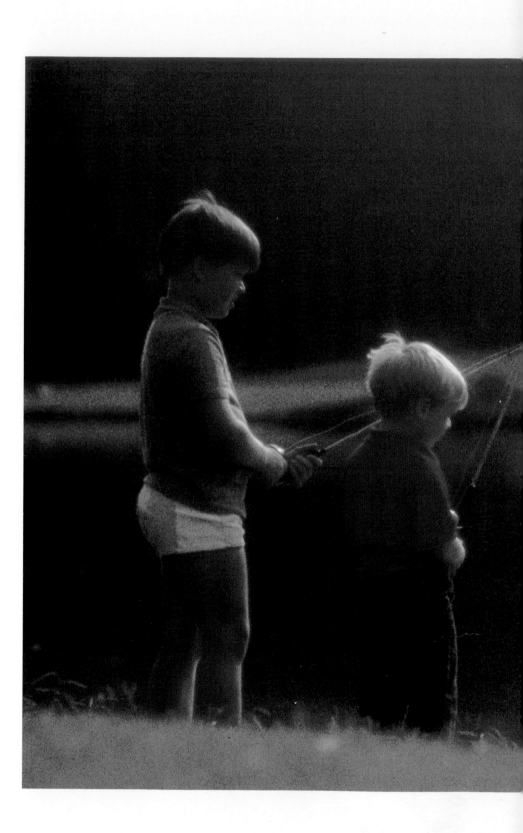

Statue of Virginia Dare,
Elizabethan Gardens, Manteo.

We know how they lived...in cottages with thatched roofs, as at home in England, in a village they called "Raleigh."

We know that children were born...the first, to Eleanor and Ananias Dare, a daughter named Virginia.

We know everything about them... except what happened to them.

Their governor, John White, went back to England for supplies. War with Spain had broken out, and he was unable to return for three long years. When he did come back, full of anxiety, he and his crew reached the north end of Roanoke Island after nightfall.

"We let fall the grapnel near the shore, and sounded the trumpet with a call...and afterward many familiar English tunes of songs... and called to them friendly. But we had no answer."

The colony was lost.

John White was sure they had merely moved.

Settlers at Jamestown years later heard stories of English families living with the Indians in the back country.

I believe they lived on. I believe their blood runs in our veins.

Roger Ball

"Here's to the land
of the longleaf pine . . .
The summer land
where the sun doth shine . . .

Where the weak grow strong
and the strong grow great.

Here's to 'down home'
—the Old North State!"

And The Strong Grow Great...

He must have been noticing people way back then, must already have been making up stories about them while he worked in Clark Porter's drug store on Elm Street in Greensboro. But of course nobody imagined that Will Porter was going to grow up to write stories the whole country would read... the ones he signed "O. Henry."

And how could anybody have known, in Asheville, that Tom, their paper boy, was a great novelist in the process of becoming? Tom—who lived with his mother at her boarding house, and walked the empty streets of the city before dawn, delivering the *Citizen* and listening to the train whistles. Thomas Wolfe never did get the train whistles out of his head.

Thomas Wolfe and his mother.

Ava Gardner.

And the little girl growing up on her father's tobacco farm at Brogden, down the road from Smithfield...the one who still has a little scar under her right eye where one of her sisters accidentally struck her with a hoe? Then she was just the youngest of the Gardner children. Ava.

This is North Carolina, where the weak grow strong and the strong grow great...and you can never be sure how great they'll grow.

Squire and Sarah Boone didn't know they were about to change the country forever when they said to their son, who was always wondering where the Yadkin River came from, "Well, Daniel, go on then, and find out."

29

Sam Ervin.   Ann Hawthorne

And people who knew the young lawyer from Waxhaw. . .who so much enjoyed the cockfights and horse races at Guilford Courthouse. . .were pretty sure Andrew Jackson was never going to amount to anything.

The Polk boy from Pineville, now he had better prospects. He was graduated first in his class from Carolina. They thought he might become a good lawyer, or even a circuit-riding judge some day.

And Jacob Johnson, janitor at the inn on Fayetteville Street in Raleigh, was said to have been right proud when his son became a tailor's apprentice in Carthage; he felt Andrew had a good career ahead of him. And he did, but not as a tailor.

The James K. Polk birthplace.

Roger Ball

Jackson, Polk and Johnson. . .each became President of the United States. The weak grow strong and the strong grow great. . . .

Tar Heels from Dolly Madison to Judge Sam Ervin have gone to Washington to put their names in the history books. . .Ed Murrow went to London. . .Kay Kyser and Andy Griffith went to Hollywood.

And some have come here from far away, looking for something in North Carolina. Hernando de Soto of Spain came to the mountains looking for gold. Carl Sandburg of Illinois came to the same mountains, looking for a quiet place to think and write.

Two brothers from Ohio came to the lonely shore, looking for a steady breeze. December 17, 1903: "After running the motor a few minutes to heat it up, I released the wire that held the machine to the track, and the machine started forward into the wind. . ." The gulls and the terns saw it. . .a curious craft of hickory sticks stuck together with Arnstein's bicycle cement. . .rising there above the sand and the sea oats.

The Wright brothers' peculiar contraption takes flight.

There is more than one kind of pioneer, of course. I think of old Washington Duke walking 150 miles back to his farm at Durham after he was mustered out of the Confederate Army, and going to work grinding tobacco with the help of his sons, Brodie and Ben and Buck. There began American Tobacco, Duke University, Duke Power and all the rest—in the motion of Washington Duke's tobacco grinder.

Here's to the land of the longleaf pine. . .home to Lincoln's mother and Whistler's mother. . .home to Dr. James E. Shepherd and Dr. Frank Porter Graham. . .to Charles Brantley Aycock and O. Max Gardner. . .to Gerald Johnson, David Brinkley and Tom Wicker of journalism. . .to the Cones of textiles, the Whites of furniture, the DeMilles of the theater. . .home to Chief Manteo. . . and you. . .and me. Great deeds were done on this land. That is prologue. Keep an eye on the paper boy, the farm girl, the dreamy-eyed kid. You're liable to hear from them later!

Washington Duke and his first tobacco factory.

North Carolina Division of Archives & History

The Farmer

"Esse Quam Videri." That is our motto. They are Latin words, but they are Tar Heel to a T. "To be rather than to seem."

The scholar who wrote that on the Great Seal of North Carolina had Virginia in mind, beyond a doubt. The Old Dominion always put on airs, and the Old North State never did.

Vain Virginia lay to the north, and smug South Carolina to the south, and North Carolina, North Carolinians said, was "a vale of humility between two mountains of conceit."

Not being proud is something North Carolinians have always been mighty proud of.

Ann Hawthorne

Well now, to tell you the truth, for a long time there, North Carolinians didn't have much *else* to be proud of. While Virginia was producing the fathers of the country—Washington, Jefferson, Madison—the families of those future Presidents, Jackson, Polk, Johnson, were moving *out* of North Carolina, looking for a better place. North Carolina was undeveloped and backward, and the average North Carolinian was a pretty rough and tumble character.

He was a simple farmer, pretty much outside the money economy, living on 50 acres or less, a crude clearing in the pine woods. He was plain in his tastes and narrow in his outlook... strong, tough, and fearless, and... I almost said hard-working... but here comes old William Byrd, traveling down from Virginia in 1728:

"Surely, there is no place in the world where people live with less labour than in North Carolina...

Joel Arrington, North Carolina Division of Travel & Tourism

"The men impose all the work upon the poor women. They make their wives rise out of their beds early in the morning, at the same time that they lie and snore, 'til the sun has run one-third of his course. Then after stretching and yawning for half an hour, they light their pipes and under the protection of a cloud of smoke, venture out into the open air. . .

"When the weather is mild, they stand leaning with both their arms upon the cornfield fence, and gravely consider whether they had best go and take a small heat at the hoe. . .but generally find reasons to put it off until another time."

William A. Bake

So there he was. . .the North Carolinian. . .as portrayed by a founder of the loftiest first family of Virginia.

Well—if this yeoman Tar Heel farmer leaning on the fence took life a little easy, you could still say this for him:

He was more self-reliant than any Virginia aristocrat. . .and more democratic than any South Carolina planter. He never did own slaves, for example, the average North Carolina farmer. He planted his crops himself. . .and harvested them himself. . .and believed himself to be the equal of any man—including any Virginian.

If I talk about the independent North Carolina farmer as if I knew him, well, I *did* know him. He was my own grandfather.

William A. Bake

41

I can see you now, John Bishop,
With your white moustaches
    tobacco-stained
And your roots so deep
    in the sand of Onslow
That you seemed as much
    a part of nature there
As the blueberries
    that grew in your ditches
And the frogs that croaked
    in your marsh
And the tall sycamore tree
    from a branch of which
You hung me a swing to swing in.

And I am swinging there now.
And you are at the woodpile
Cutting heart pine into kindling,
The short arc of your sharp ax
Sending a perfect splinter
    of golden wood
Cartwheeling away
    from the chopping block
With every perfect stroke.

And now Rena Bishop,
Good-hearted woman,
    my grandmother,
Her hair tied as it always was
    in a knot behind her head,
And carrying a cooking pot,
Opens the screen door to come
    to the pump on the porch
For water in which to cook
    the butter beans for supper
On the woodstove in the kitchen.
And she puts down the pot and
    wipes her hands on her apron
And smiles to see me swinging.
She was a teacher and lover of books
Who earned the love of many children,
And especially of me.

Hugh Morton

*Rena Bishop, Charles Kuralt's
grandmother.*

And I swing so high that I can see
The watering trough, the corn crib,
   the unpainted barn,
The shed under the hayloft from
   which we moved the wagon
   into the yard
To make room for the Chevrolet.
And I swing so high that I can see
The mule in the pasture,
Old Red,
With a mean reputation.
Rarely hitched to the wagon now,
   only to the plow,
For you cannot use a Chevrolet to
   plow a furrow.
And there are the two cows, drowsy
   on their feet,
And there are the two pigs sleeping
   in the mud.

And there is the picket fence,
Whitewashed once upon a time,
Surrounding the twisted apple trees,
And the ripe smell of apples
   on the ground.
And there is the smokehouse,
Enclosing the moldy smell of hams
   and dirt and brine.

William A. Bake

45

William A. Bake

And I swing so high that I can see
Down the sandy road to the field of green tobacco,
To the tilted tobacco barn,
Logs hand-squared and chinked with mud
Where I stayed up half the night with you, John Bishop,
During curing time,
Listening in the darkness to the quiet talk
Of the men around the fire,
Drinking, manfully, like you,
From the gourd dipper that hung by a string from the
     water bucket.
And feeling gratified when you asked my opinion,
Gravely,
Of whether the heat in the curing barn was staying even.

And I swing so high that I can see
Into the windows of the room on the second floor
Where I blew out the kerosene lamp
To sleep through the cold nights,
Blissfully,
Under a pile of quilts in the tall feather bed.
And woke in the cold mornings
To splash cold water from the basin onto my face,
And then rush down the stairs in my underwear,
Past the cold front rooms,
Past the cold parlor used only for weddings and funerals
And Christmas,
Past the front door, used never,
Into the warm kitchen
To get dressed amid the smells of breakfast cooking.

What is a childhood memory for me
Was a life for you, John Bishop.
I see you sink your ax
    into the chopping block
And stoop to collect the kindling
    on the ground.
And I, no longer interested
    in swinging,
Come running barefoot,
Because I am sure
You need my help.

You were a plain man,
Able, dignified and kind,
Learned in many things,
    though not in Latin.
Your epitaph, however,
Is there, on the Great Seal, in Latin:

"Esse Quam Videri."

The Barbecue Blues

The waiter brought the champagne
    and discreetly popped the cork
In a fancy French restaurant on the east side of New York.
The patron sipped it glumly with his caviar soufflé;
I could see his heart was heavy, and his mind was far away.
He said: "I was raised on black-eyed peas and barbecue,
    And butter beans and turnip greens
        and brunswick stew.
    And every time I drink champagne, I yearn
    For buttermilk from Grandma's butter churn."

Bruce Roberts

Then they served his pâté from the liver of a goose.

Then they served his quiche Lorraine and his chocolate mousse,

When they brought his cognac, he just shook his head

And looked at me in sadness, and this is what he said.

He said: "I was fed on cracklin' bread and country hams

            And sausage meat and hominy and candied yams.

            I have dined on all the world's cuisines;

            I wish I had me a mess of collard greens."

He said his butler always serves him breakfast in bed.

Said he orders buttermilk biscuits and gets croissants instead.

Said they give him Belgian waffles no matter how he begs

For country ham, ham gravy, grits and eggs.

He said: "Now excuse me, friend, but tears come to my eyes

            Each time I think about my Mama's apple pies

            And sourwood honey from my Papa's hives.

            Oh, sometimes men leave home and ruin their lives!"

He said: "Friend, you get awful tired of Brie.

If you're goin' down home, tell 'em this for me.

Just one thing, tell 'em, I implore ya.

They don't serve chicken and dumplin's in the Waldorf Astoria."

He said: "Oh I've had those escargots that they serve in France.

            You pay your francs and give your thanks and take
                your chance.

            And when I eat lasagna down in Rome,

            I'm thinkin' 'bout that livermush back at home!"

Then he nodded to the waiter and sadly paid his bill
And took his leave of me. And I can see him still
With his head bowed down as he wandered forth . . .
A Tar Heel starving in the North.
He said: "Now I'm eating sturgeon eggs they serve on toast,
And thinkin' 'bout the good food that I want the most,
Like barbecue and roasted ears of corn
From that North Carolina farm where I was born!"

55

Young folks, think on that man's folly,
Before you board that bus in Raleigh
And head north for fame and fortune.
Just beware. . .
They have limousines
      and designer jeans
And diamond rings
      and such-like things. . .
But there's *nothing* to *eat* up there!

Clay Nolen, North Carolina Division of Travel & Tourism

*B*ackroads & Byways. . .
I have been to Farmer, Friendship, Franklin and Fountain, N.C., and gazed upon most of the creeks and peaks and county seats named in the following bit of doggerel, but I'd never have been able to remember them all without the assistance of Professor William S. Powell's formidable book *The North Carolina Gazetteer,* published by the University of North Carolina Press. Therein are named all the North Carolina communities and geographical features existent, and many that existed once upon a time but no longer. I browsed through that miraculous book for hours. I pronounce it the Ultimate Literary Achievement of North Carolina, more evocative than *Look Homeward, Angel* and a lot more fun.

I hated having to leave out Rabbit Shuffle, N.C., not to mention Airbellows and Stiffknee Knob and Coldass Creek. . .all places Bill Powell chronicled and I had never heard of. . .but I couldn't make any of them rhyme. I found, however, that many of our state's place names fall naturally into a lyrical meter, obviously meant to be sung. All together, now:

Hickory, Dickerson, Dockery, Dunn

Peckerwood Ridge and Poorhouse Run!

William A. Bake

AHO RD >

Up there in Watauga County, at the head of Buffalo Creek, there's a little place called Aho. Years ago, some of the men who lived there met around a stove to decide what to call the place, and they couldn't agree. . . but they couldn't stay all night either. . . so after considering dozens of names, to which one or another of them raised an objection, they decided the next name out of anybody's mouth would become the name of their community. They sat there a while in silence. . . until Mr. B. B. Dougherty stood up and stretched himself and said, "Ahhh-ho." That's how Aho, North Carolina, got its name.

Farmer. Friendship. Franklin. Fountain.

Bullfrog Creek and Burntshirt Mountain.

Along in the late 1800's, they decided to put a new post office in rural Randolph County, and of course the post office had to be called something, so the people of the community fell to discussing it. Why not call it this, why not call it that? Somebody said, "Why not call it Whynot?" And that's the name to this day. Why not?

Yadkin. Yancey. Yorick. York.

Ripshin Ridge and Roaring Fork!

Far from home, my mind embraces
the nimble names of Tar Heel Places:

Topsail Sound and Turner's Cut
Dixon and Vixen and Devil's Gut.
Hoke, Polk, Ashe, Nash.
Calico. Calabash.
Pitt. Hyde. Clay. Dare.
Cape Fear. Cat Square.

Take me home to Teaches Hole,
To Looking Glass Creek,
        and Frying Pan Shoal,
To Bridal Veil and Blowing Rock...
And Currituck and Coinjock.

I'll know I'm home when I finally reach
The top of a dune at Wrightsville Beach
And stand there
        with my back to the sea

Looking west toward Cherokee
And imagining the miles between...
        From Ivanhoe to Aberdeen,
    Candor and Biscoe, Uwharrie
    To Gold Hill, Granite Quarry
    China Grove and Cullowhee.

Miles farther than a man can see
Except in the eye of his memory.

Turkey Den, Tally Ho, Dora's Mills.

Chinquapin, Pamlico, Kill Devil Hills.

Jennie Lind. Chasm Prong.

Laudermilk Bend. Scuppernong.

Polecat, Possumtrot,

Pop Castle, Porter.

Swannanoa. Swan Quarter.

Sly. Slosh. Shoe. Small.

Rumbling Bald. Rural Hall.

Lizard Lick and Licklog Gap.

Level Cross. Old Trap.

Snow Camp. Silverstone.

Worm Creek. Whalebone.

Snead's Ferry, Spruce Pine.

Shoofly. Sunshine.

Latter-day North Carolinians have erased some of the good old names from the map, dignified them a little, you know. Hog Quarter is called Spot now, and Taggard's Mill is now Whispering Pines. Sounds better to the Chamber of Commerce. When somebody started a mill on the Smith River in 1813, they called the place *Splashy* for the water the mill wheel threw up. By the time I came along, they had modified that to *Spray. Spray* sounded more genteel than *Splashy.* Then they got a Chamber of Commerce and of course you know what they call the place now: *Eden!*

Eden is a good enough name for a place, and very elementary, but I think I'd rather plant my apple tree in *Splashy.*

Many of the old names are still there on our land.

Jim Dumbell, *The Charlotte Observer*

Saxapahaw, Waxhaw, Kennakeet.

Ocracoke, Roanoke and Mattamuskeet.

Tony, Toddy, Topsy, Trent...

I wonder which Peggy the old-timers meant
When they named that hilltop Peggy Peak?
And who was the Patchet of Patchet's Creek?

Granny Green Mountain is a place I've seen...
Where have you gone to, Granny Green?
There are towns called Martha
    and Mamie and Mollie.
Who *were* they? What happened
    at Lockwood's Folly?

I know a crossroads named Loafer's Glory
Oh, how I'd love to know *that* story!
To have *met* the loafers, to have known their faces,
To know *all* the stories of the Tar Heel places...

Maiden Cane. Castle Hayne. Camp Lejeune.

Walters Mill. Weaverville. Bonnie Doone.

Who was the man
    who had the temerity
To name his town, sincerely, Sincerity?
It's smaller, but no sincerer
    than Raleigh . . .
Or Mabel or Martha or Mamie
    or Mollie!

Exotic names on the
    signposts stand . . .
Warsaw and Sparta and Samarkand!
They're not a bit like the cities for
    which they're named . . .
You'd have thought Tar Heels might
    have been shamed
To change it from Splashy
    to Spray to *Eden* . . .
But it came from the literature
    they'd been readin'
And it sounded nice,
    and they weren't a bit coy. . . .

Inside the Mast Store, Valle Crucis.

And where is Carthage?
Right down the road from Troy!

Badin and Ayden
and Maiden and Wise.

Ranger, Granger, Angier and Spies.

Dallas, Frisco and Providence, too.

Now where is the town
that's home to you?

Minnesott?

Why not?

WHYNOT

69

*D*inner On The Grounds

On every dusty road in North Carolina, there stands a white frame church, looking as if it's always been there. But it hasn't been.

Before 1800, not one North Carolinian in 30 belonged to a church. Tar Heels were too busy scrimping for a living to be bothered with preachers in pulpits telling them how to live. Toward most religion they were apathetic, and toward the "established" Anglican Church downright antipathetic. Even the Scotch-Irish, nominally Presbyterians, were described as people who "kept God's Commandments—and every other good thing they could get their hands on."

That was North Carolina—before the Baptists got here!

Charles Gupton, Southern Light

When the preacher finally says the last Amen

Church is over and that's when we begin

Spreadin' that table, under the trees

Shakin' the cloth out, fanning the Sunday breeze

Appetites ready, knowing no bounds

'Cause today we're having dinner on the grounds.

The Baptists...Free Will Baptists, Primitive Baptists, Separate Baptists... preaching the gospel from any rough platform or tree stump, brought religion home to every crossroads. And not only the Baptists, but also the circuit-riding Methodist preachers, ready with three hours of powerful oratory for wherever they had ridden to by Sunday. And the red gullies of the Piedmont echoed the Welsh chants. And the Sandhills rang with the Scots accents of the great old Presbyterian orators. And there were Moravians proclaiming the word of God in old German. There were austere Anglicans...and modest Quakers...but there were Baptists most of all!

Roger Ball

Papa's pourin' ice tea in each Dixie cup.

Hungry children are the first ones lining up,

Looking for Mama's chocolate cake.

Where are those fried pies only Aunt Sue can make?

Fanning the flies off, scatter them hounds,

'Cause today we're having dinner on the grounds.

And people from miles around would go to wherever the preaching was to be that Sunday. . .ride in their farm carts. . .or walk barefoot, carrying their shoes so they could be clean shod when they got there. Some of the preachers became famous and their preaching became a rural recreation. And then and there in that Great Revival of long ago, was born the hallowed social custom of all day preaching and dinner on the grounds!

Thank the good Lord for the bountiful supply,

Say the blessing and grab some apple pie.

Get a cold biscuit, fill it with ham

Reach for the pickles next to the candied yams.

Pickin' up chicken, pickin' up pounds,

Cause today we're having dinner on the grounds.

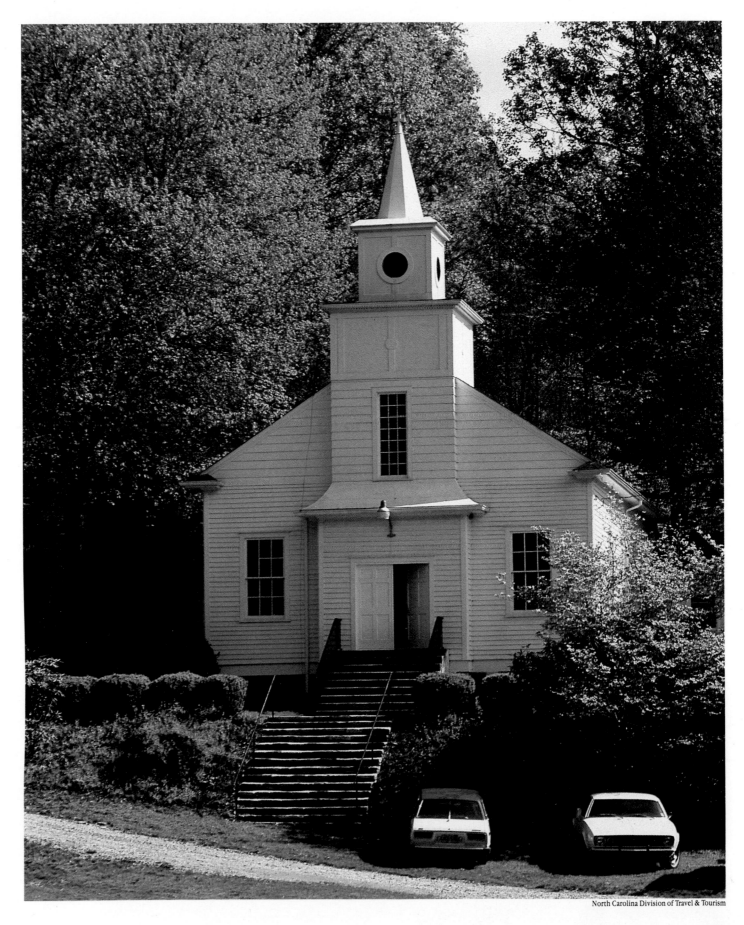

And if one long day of preaching and singing and socializing was good for the soul, *seven* days was *seven* times better. In Lincoln County, on the banks of the Catawba, there stands a grove of ancient oak trees which have shaded the tents of the week-long Rock Springs Methodist Camp Meeting for 150 summers and more. . .and will do so next summer and every summer until the last hymn is forgotten and human fellowship no longer valued.

If you're passin' by the church
        on picnic day,
You're invited to come
        right in and stay
Under the shade trees,
        plenty to eat,
Plenty of nice folks
        you'll be glad to meet.
Happy occasion,
        laughter abounds
'Cause today we're having
        dinner on the grounds.
                    Amen.

A "Singing on the Mountain."

Hugh Morton

First There Was A Dulcimer. . .

"How many biscuits can you eat?
"Forty-nine and a ham of meat,
"This mornin', this evenin', right now!"

Those were the exquisite words, lustily sung, of the sign-on tune of the Briarhoppers. The Briarhoppers were the Juilliard String Quartet of country music, and theirs was the music of my youth and upbringing in North Carolina. I thought *all* music on this earth was played by guitar, banjo, fiddle and bass, for that is pretty much all we ever heard on WBT radio.

The Briarhoppers.

(opposite page) Ed Presnell, famed dulcimer maker.

Those country bands were the amplified lineal descendants of the restless Scotch-Irish who wandered down into the Carolina mountains from Pennsylvania in the 18th Century, bringing their songs with them, work songs, drinking songs, lullabies and hymns.

There were songs about Buffalo Gals and Old Gray Mares, and always, always about Careless Love.

They plug the guitars into an electric socket these days, but the theme of Careless Love won't go away. The great William T. Polk of Greensboro wrote of this music:

> "The songs are good and evil, sweet and mean, solemn and funny, beautiful and ugly; there are spirituals and there are devil ditties; they are all that people are; they are ourselves."

Doc Watson.

With a mountain dulcimer playing in the background, then, and Doc Watson humming "Down in the Valley," for this is the true origin of our North Carolina music-making, let us allow that there were Tar Heels who listened to different drummers, and who felt altogether different rhythms welling up inside them.

There were the black gospel singers, rattling the rafters of the country churches; when Shirley Caesar of Durham thrills people all over the world with her gospel songs, she is giving them a pure North Carolina thrill.

There were the jazz singers and players, some of whom went on to greatness. Shall we mention Dizzy Gillespie, who went to school in Laurinburg? Shall we name John Coltrane and Roberta Flack? Nina Simone of Tryon, Dr. Billy Taylor of Greenville, Thelonius Monk of Rocky Mount? Jazz music, the only original American art, and the richest, was made richer by far by a few

Roger Ball

Dizzy Gillespie.

original North Carolinians. Everybody knows that tobacco and textiles and furniture are North Carolina's great exports. Well, there's one other, as hot and smoky as any burning cigarette, as rich and detailed as any fabric, and as well-crafted as any armchair or divan. It is jazz music, and some of the best originated right here.

There were the band leaders who rose to prominence in the time of the "big bands." For a while there in the Forties and Fifties, *most* of them seemed to come from North Carolina—Kay Kyser and Skinnay Ennis, Les Brown, John Scott Trotter, Johnny Long and Hal Kemp.

There were giants of the concert stage, native-born and internationally applauded, among them Norman Cordon, the Metropolitan Opera star; Thor Johnson, the symphony orchestra conductor; and Lamar Stringfield, the Pulitzer Prize-winning composer.

And never before in North Carolina's 400 years of music—from the English lute to the electronic synthesizer—has there been so much toe-tapping, horn-playing and close harmony as there is in the state right now. On any given night, North Carolinians have their choice of a grass roots opera, a chamber recital, a symphony concert, a jazz performance, an oratorio program, a Singing on the Mountain, a hymn service, a fiddling convention or a square dance. The songs are "good and evil, sweet and mean, solemn and funny...they are ourselves."

Mountain Sampler

If a man's from the mountains, he'll tell you. If he's not, why embarrass him by asking?

Doree Pitkin

🍂 I'd rather be a knot on a log up here on Grandfather than have to live down at Colletsville.

William A. Bake

🍂 Oh, this is good strong land. It must be, to hold up all the rocks we got around here.

(opposite page) Ginseng gatherer.

93

🍂 And mountain living is easy living. When your pumpkins are ripe and you've grabbled out your potatoes, all you have to do is start 'em and they'll roll right down into your kitchen.

Warren Moore

🍂 Here's to old corn likker. . .whitens the teeth, perfumes the breath, and makes childbirth a pleasure. What does it taste like? It tastes like a lighted kerosene lantern. . .or two cats fightin' in your mouth. Does it improve with age? Well, I kept a quart jar of it a week one time, and I couldn't tell that it was one bit better than when it was new and fresh.

Ann Hawthorne

🍂 Oh, yes, I've got religion. I believe it's a sin to feed chickens on Sunday. I feed mine on corn.

🍂 There was a circuit-riding preacher come up this holler one time. He asked my neighbor-lady was there any Presbyterians around here. She said, "Well, Pa did kill some kind of varmint, and nailed his hide to the back of the shed. You can go see if that's one."

Patty Davis

Warren Moore

🍂 Well, what's your hurry, stranger? Light and come in if you can get in for all the plunder here on the porch.

Come in and set a spell.

Hugh Morton

NORTH CAROLINA IS MY HOME

words by Charles Kuralt

music by Loonis McGlohon

Car - o - li - na raised me straight as a moun - tain pine, _____

Rocked me in her cra - dle, South - ern moth - er mine. _____

North Car - o - li - na is my home, ___ Home far be - yond all ___

praise, Good - li - est home un - der Heav - en's dome,

Here I shall spend my days. _____